Night Chorus

Night Chorus

Many ~
Best Wishes ~
Joani Reese

Joani Reese

Cover Art: Night Chorus
by Lisa Cardenas © 2015

ISBN: 978-1-943170-02-9

Cover Design: Jane L. Carman
Interior Design: Paige Domantey
Production Director: Jane L. Carman

Typefaces: Garamond and Apple Chancery

Published by: Lit Fest Press, Carman, 688 Knox Road 900 North, Gilson, Illinois
61436

festivalwriter.org

For Mychael and Danny
This is the way we sail toward land

Table of Contents

I. Overture

II. Verismo

III. Motif

IV. Vibrato

V. Intermezzo

VI. Adagio

VII. Coda

I. Overture

The Poem

Reach for it outside muscle, blood, and bone,
beyond the small, precise cut; though painful,
the blood on the page is precious only to you.
Encompass the world in a word, no cracked

leather heels that betray poverty, not tumorous
drunks scenting a Bowery alley. Please,
no snowy peaks syruped in sunlight,
not even *Popocatépetl*, banking its flames.

Instead, offer the seduction of apocalypse.
Unearth the beating heart of an Aztec virgin.
It's not about the firefly's demise in a sugar-sticky hand,
nor an arm, wavering, blue beneath the ice crusted

waters of Lake Michigan, No. It's not about death,
the dying father-—certainly not about love,
loss. Instead, language must eclipse mourning,
ignore the hyacinth's breath and the feathered rose.

Words must transcend the experience of the eye,
—offer new vistas to the jaded
who already know the color of the sky.

Put Down Your Camera and Love Me

The dead whale's bones wash to white
on the beachhead in Puerto Peñasco.
We are full of chalupas, salsa verde,
and bad Mexican music. Your mouth

tastes of sea salt, the margaritas
we drank at the fish market bar.
I take a swallow, taste lime,
drink you in.

The skeletal shadow sinks eastward.
Twinned porpoise streak silver over the sea.
Sunset fingers through the carcass
to touch a tourist who stops to snap
a photo of his future.

Play

Remove the silver slippers and slip them in a pocket safe from sin.
Your slip slides against silken skin as you climb the slippery stairs
of the child's slide to slide down until your toes touch tawny sand.
Slip between the swings and sunset surf to take another sip of gin.
Try to fill the hollow space inside your chest that harbors hidden grief.
A lie slid off your tongue to leave you single, standing solo here below
the slanted sun. A sweet and slippery stranger slides aside your slip
with hands so soft you barely even notice you are lost.

Playa Encanto

The first morning we wake, trucks shower water
to bind the red dust to the road. Only beach grass
and ice plant survive on the bluffs of Encanto.
We unpack our suitcases, boxes of food,
then begin our ritual walk along the sand.
Danny spies a shimmering shape near the water.
Moving closer, we see a baby dolphin rocking
in the swell, its mouth full of bacterial scum. It rolls
on the tide. An open eye points to heaven; its neck gapes,
slit by fishnet or gaff. Perhaps it was Alejandro
with the golden incisor who sells knock-off Brighton bags
when shrimp aren't plentiful. His stall on Calle Principal
offers shell necklaces and strings of sea horse cadavers
at a very good price. Steel-blue skin peels from the slash.
Color shines from the revealed gash: yellow, almost pretty,
like the guayaba we slipped between our lips at breakfast.
Its belly oozes a second wound, sculpted like a smile.
Danny drops his skim board and gentles the body
onto higher sand. Entrails slip from the slit and whirl
in the surf. Blood christens Danny's beach shoes
then is washed away by the waves. His face turns
from me: a little boy who thinks he's too old for tears,
with questions to ask, but answers aren't easy.
We float the baby back to deep water, bury it
beneath Encanto's waves.

The Human Condition

It's what sets us apart,
the thin film of dust borne on the tongue
we can never quite wash away,
those microscopic filaments that grow
earthward from our soles with each step we take.
The knowledge that gravity will root us, finally
and forever, in the clay beneath our feet
is why we teach our children
how to dance.

Ophelia

She fabricates life in a lamp-lit room,
cloaks herself in poetry, in the singing
of this poem. Ophelia considers company
but decides to go it alone.

It begins: The tube snakes slowly inside.
She watches a plane knife through clouds
beyond the clinic's window. A plastic jar fills
with one perfect white sucking sound.

Another infant girl or boy unknown.
The nurse hovers, lowers her gown, says,
"All that could have been is undone."
It is a good saying, she thinks, *it is true.*

In the evening as the sun fades to brown,
Ophelia invites her friends and her friends' friends
to wash the color from her hands,
some with whiskey, some with wine.

She lingers beside the river, feet bare on rocks,
anxious to touch the water, to return. God
is not in heaven. He is in motion, a copper creature
bearing down, determined to find the name

without a sound. Ophelia dives, secret gripped
in a palm. Turned loose, it swims and flickers
in the dusky wash of half-light, then is gone.

To a Husband, Once Removed

I've settled in Lampasas, Texas, just outside Killeen.
Driving the U-Haul, I passed a line of staggered hills stacked
like angry chins; they angled north toward the town
of Retribution where I stopped for a time.

After I reached Lampasas, I found a cabin on a back road.
The owners threw in some red curtains, a velvet Elvis,
and a black Naugahyde sofa. A pine desk rests
under a window that pearls with evening light.

The Congregation of Jesus Our Star-crossed Savior,
is wired for sound. The cupola beams Revelation
to sinners and saints from its peak forty feet above the ground
and drowns out the jukebox in the Yellow Rose Cafe.

Most evening's, static gospel music covers the town
like a coat of pea-green paint. Hank, the bartender
at Moody's Saloon says I can get saved any Sunday at noon
or Wednesday evenings when I'm ready to see the light.

Some days I walk at sunrise, watch live oak shadows
expand over the tacky gumbo natives here call dirt.
I follow uncertain directions without dread. I've walked
down such dubious paths before.

At dusk, the sky inflates and preens in gunmetal blue.
I carry my Chablis outside and sit on the porch or lean against the rail.
I try to find sadness for the muddy river and all those pretty things
I left behind. I suspect they still survive. I guess I will too.

The buffalo grass I planted grows slowly; I till beneath the Texas sun
and wonder how it continues at all. Always thirsty, it tufts the thick clay,
leaves spaces I never seem able to fill. My cabin's on a rural route;
it has no mailbox or visible address. Don't come. Don't call.

I searched today through thorned mesquite and purple sage
for something that I thought I'd lost. Prairie dogs bolted
through the scrub nearby; some stood upright, chittering
their anger at me. We either fight or run away.

I found a wild rose outside the fence and transplanted it to a garden
I've begun—Too soon to tell if it's damaged and won't survive.
Sometimes, when it looks as though something will die,
it surprises and offers a flower or two.

A Thousand Days

It's so much more respectable to drown
one's woes beneath the channel's oily sheen.
I never should have married for a crown.

The tower's chill. I pace from stone to stone,
my throne a threadbare carpet, and it seems
it's so much more respectable to drown.

My daughter has her father's hair. She's known
to be a legal heir. I hope she yearns
to marry *no one*, even for a crown.

Some claim my brother lay with me, I own
it's possible, but not whilst I was queen—
It's so much more respectable to drown.

Lord Cromwell's stock is rising like the sun,
his stealthy machinations slipped between
King Henry and myself. I've lost the crown.

The swordsman from Calais, whose stroke is clean,
will part me from my life for Lady Jane.
It's so much more respectable to drown.
I never should have married for a crown.

Vignette for Spring

April shakes winter's hollow limbs beyond the screen.
Poplar branches clatter and brittle in pieces
to lie shattered on the lane. Shun the narcissus;
its yellow coronas trumpet the lie of resurrection.

A lover you will never meet passes by
hair struck silver under the mounting sun.
His gaze points toward heaven. The red of his lips
goes forever unkissed. A mandolin laughs from a window.

Somewhere, a vibrating string snaps to startle the ear.

Evanescence

Eyes wide beside you, I trace the path
of headlights from slick roadways
beyond the glass. It is 2am.

No waxing swell of moon presses
its yellow ribbons through cracks
to aid my vision. The air is weary

tonight. The streetlight blooms
over your profile, then flickers and dies.
Instead of sheep, I count the silences

between us. You turn your back to me
in sleep. My palm hovers, feels warmth
rise from your sheeted form, withdraws

Midlife

The summer disappeared too quickly
and yet the light still burns the hills
these late afternoons for far too long.
Our hands grow smaller. We've learned,
finally, not to reach beyond ourselves.
We resemble one another
but cannot reassemble the lovers
who have vanished. Each evening,
we speak with bright razors
stashed beneath our tongues, slash
toward each other's jugular, cut
new wounds to expose the blood rush
that gratifies but can never replace desire.

Touch

If you are,
then find me.
Drowning,
underwater,
sluice wasted time
away.

Find me
reading shadows
rocking astride
empty words
and neverhours.

If you breathe
then breathe me
away from night
to light again.

There is a touch
below the belly
that feeds
unsated flesh.
Believe.

Burn clean
cleave to bone,
pubis, slick, lost.
Open me.

One glance
from you
might spawn
passion, might
finish me.

If you are
this instant
then find me.

Abstinence

I've sipped for days to slake a thirst
I never thought I'd have again.

Each day I wake as currents thrum
through blood and flesh, untempered heart.

I banish flame—swallow the truth,
dispatch it to a southern sky,

and still my longing burns your likeness
in his dark and watchful eyes.

II. Verismo

No Bees Please

Her poetry: all about Otto,
his entomology, his absence.
Write me a one-eyed daisy,
stamen stroked by buzzing tongues,
busy in their Electra-like desire.

Postmodern Peanut Butter Sandwich

Expose him, the first thief
who culled the strange fruit,
plundered heartwood
from another man's tree.
Blue hues, strained through blank,
brittle pages of Baptist bibles
poured over an ivory palate
to pack the cotton panties
of pubescent girls—with a bullet.

Cunning Iago with pompador'd fin,
a hillbilly hipster humping heartbreak
in roadhouse finery. Nothing intrinsic
ever flowed to the North,
save a white boy whose mouth dripped
of sweat-leather sex steeped
in Tupelo breast milk and honey.

Memphis' man. Androgy's scam.
Colonel Tom's Cadillac King.
The slick highway man
polished *That's All Right Mama*,
rubbed her clean,
and drove her to Levittown, steamroll'd
over Hoboken, sang gospel 'til dawn,

whitewashed Vegas
with feather brushes plucked
from a black man's swansong.
Blind Willie's voice lies intestate,
while his tunes transcend solid gold.

Dear John

The music plays on, my friend.
These new wars, like yours,
spend ripe bodies like pocket change
and do not end. You reach out
to Imagine us, thirty-one years on
as we trip along, skin our knees
against the hard surface
of absolute belief, still as solipsistic
and content as spotted cats,
self-grooming in the sun.

Resurrection

On the third day
Hemingway would probably reconstruct
his ruined head like pieces of a jigsaw puzzle
then ease down the snow belted Ketchum road.
Kicking a can, he'd stroll into the next decade
dragging the severed rack of a ten point buck,
in search of another clean, well-lighted place.

Like a film strip run backward, Berryman's fingertips
might glance the dewed bank as he ascends feet first
to the Washington Avenue bridge. Mistress Bradstreet
would take his hand, lead him to the nearest podium,
his Pulitzer pressed under an arm, a new poem
scarifying patterns in his boozy brain.

Crane, velvet bathrobe billowing behind,
wavers on the prow, his tented hands lifted
to the Mexican sky. He steps back from the abyss,
inner eye envisioning the ink sip of a fountain pen,
the hard, hot brain frenzy that sends phrases marching
toward another bridge between oblivion and art.

Sexton could reduce her carbon footprint, wait
for a newer model, one in candy apple red with doll's eyes
winking from the radio dials while Plath entwines
with Otto in the back seat. The three could motor east,
race to beat the rising sun, anxious to be the first
to see the angel roll back the stone.

Soir Bleu

—after a painting by Edward Hopper

Pierrot and his cigarette are out of place.
Hanging from rouged lips, the Gauloise remains forever unlit;
white and pure like the greasepaint that masks his flesh.
He is afraid watchers think him unmanly.
His eyes burn inside red diamonds.
Look closely;
the ruff around his neck is stained with sweat
and street dust. His hairless skull
is painted too. He ignores his woe to drink.

A thick palette of rouge and lipstick cannot hide
his woman's age, although she thinks it does, a little.
She knows his needs; knows he likes her helpless
on her knees in the blue night. Sometimes, he pulls her
by the hair, presses her mouth against him.
He will pay her in fists pulled from pockets
of trousers he never removes.

His two companions, black beret, white epaulets,
do not wish to finish the wine and go home.
Their wives are fat, their children hungry and dirty.
The companions speak the patois of the street;
share coarse stories, and women.
Their laughter is a lie.
A fourth carafe of Chablis sits half-empty
on the table, a fifth will come.

Children laugh at this clown;
Nannies toss coins at his feet; Dogs growl and nip.
No one knows his dreams are suffused with night
— the greasepaint hides it all.
His woman waits in silence to his right.
Later, he will force her

to the hard floor, her mouth a slash of red.
This thought, perhaps, makes him grin.

She has blackened the gray from her hair,
its angular cut frames raw cheekbones.
A last pair of earrings sparkle from her lobes.
Her arms are white, thick; her breasts
heave from a green bodice.
The tilt of her chin begs an answer
a clown can never give.

A Letter from Your Sisters

Dear Sylvia and Anne:
We are stuck in your confessional.
We can't get out. The marriage
of outhouse noise with barnyard pig-grunts
stuffs our ears with ugliness.
You sculpted your pain onto each page,
gaining speed and direction
like the terminal thrusts of a rejected lover.
You knew time was short, the long night
creeping inside your heads. Yet you sought
no creaking door, no key, no light
to seep through cracks and direct your retreat
from the edge. The air crackles,
alive with electro-shock. We turn
and we turn our feet, retrace each step
believed to have led us here
where everything known vanishes.
We smell carbon monoxide and cooking gas
as a bloody sun slips slowly
into a mulberry sea.

Blues Note

Saxophone notes stroke the bricks
on Beale. A black man hands love
a melody, plays the music of ghosts.
Voices echo over the midnight street.
The couple stops. A girl sways and drops
dollars in the open case crouching
at the bluesman's feet.

The man grasps her elbow and steers
west, beyond the street lights where stars
pearl the Mississippi's breast. Her body
plunges to become a creature of filtered light
as delta mud swirls beneath the currents.
He wipes a jackknife clean against the earth
and sends it toppling after her.

Sinking beneath the broken line of entry,
blonde braids waver; a hand drifts skyward
through water threaded red around a face.
Poised just south of day, a mother
in Potontoc County sleeps. Before she wakes,
she dreams of dark hands, of blue notes swirling
on Memphis air, of a daughter's bourbon
loneliness, of her little girl with braided,
silken hair.

Storm

Nimbus scrape their claws over the bluffs and growl. A body
is transformed by purpose into muscle and sinew.
She maneuvers over rocks to embrace the onrushing storm,
gone too far to retrace the steps that led here. The summit
peaks just ahead. She rises, a white flag above the Mississippi.
Fingers peel and discard rags of the past, tatters of colorful cloth
slide away on the wind. A wedding ring rattles down the slope,
plunges through the water below. She teeters, naked on the cliff edge,
wild sky black. Arms spread, she dives through the terrible rain.

Schadenfreude

The spider perches high in her God's-eye web,
abdomen flashing yellow and black.
Unskeined silk frames early jewels of dew.
She will feast on the careless,
those who have not learned there is danger
in such beauty. Woven shrouds wave
between tender branches, stilled wings
fixed fast to tiny bodies as she feeds.

Oh, Hell

First you die in August or some other month
or someone kills you in Detroit; the Galapagos.
your driveway; your dreams, or you drown. But
you don't rack up points for how it happens.
Or when. Or why. Even if you suffered.
No points. No one cares. No donut.

Then you see this woman. Funky red horns
look phalically familiar—Some kind of tail.
 She waves a flowered bow tie.
A searchlight extends from her forehead.
A can of spray paint clutched between her thighs,
she points a jeweled fingernail at the wall.
You stroll, read tags from the Koran, *Tora! Tora! Tora!*
Mein Kampf, Lassie, The Gnostic Gospels and
Tender Buttons in Day-Glo orange and pink.
There is a tunnel. A sign reads,
"Gemillut Chassadim, Do Not Go This Way,"
so you don't.

A bald Hindu lawyer wearing *Pampers*
imprinted with wireless spectacles
spreads his arms to block a smoked glass door
behind which you glimpse a party going on.
He smiles. His mouth swallows his head.
You eye the submarines, want to crawl inside,
become one with shredded lettuce, mayo, Swiss cheese.
No nukes here, no triage, no wounded to nurse, or shoot.
You lick your finger, taste day-old codfish.

A stroll to the gift shop bends each minute
like a Dali watch as you wait to get this trip straight
with the ticket machine. There are pens
with red laser lights, Betty Crocker Devil's Food
cake mix, pickled jalapenos, golden nipple rings

and Ball jars filled with Ass-Kickin' Chili.
Bob Marley stands too close to you,
a red-eared slider perches like a yarmulke on his head.
He speaks through lips dangling a massive spliff,
"Do not lose *your* head, you are not really here."

Spike Lee, caped like Zorro, struts over the threshold,
his left arm draped around Lina Wertmuller.
Lina feeds a dog-eared copy of *Swept Away*
By An Unusual Destiny in the Blue Sea of August
into his mouth. She tugs Spike's mustache
because Giancarlo Gianini is not here to make her laugh.
She has strung blue eyes and rabbit's feet
from a chain around her neck

Spike hands you these things—
A metal pail with sides that rainbow
like trout flanks under water, overflowing
with stone crabs from Joe's and spiked hands,
a black leather Laker's cap,
and a rather curt note —from God.
The postscript scrawled across the bottom
in number two pencil reads,
"Must have missed your connection, dude.
Have a nice stay."

III. Motif

Now

I hear the past
being dragged across the heart
pine floor for hours and hours.
When its screech of protest
ends, I'm afraid to move
into the next room,
wary of the scars
its weight has carved,
the deep cuts in soft wood
that will ooze beneath
my naked feet, the
splinters left behind.
This thought is heavy;
and staggers under its own heft.
Stay with me tonight and dance,
safe from the ruin
beyond these bolted doors.

Eve

Her story, history, hysterectomy, hysteria
Vagina, vaginal, virginal, magical, genital
Practical, primal, pudendal, pudere
Prisoner, mystery, memento mori
Purgatory, purged, plumed, illumined
Blamed, inflamed, doomed, shamed, medicated
Meditate, salivate, masturbate, bait, berate
Bloom, woman, womb, dumb, rubber
Rule, abuse, use, uterus, neuter us, nakedness
Fake, hate, flagellate, instigate, infiltrate
Subjugate, crooked, straight, bait, berate
Bare, stare, swear, player, prayer
Amen, semen, menstruate, specimen
Circumcise, infantilize, circumstance
Circle, circus, beatus, bellus, ballus, sellus
Puerile, sterile, stereotype, rape, rope
Scrape, rate, rut, runt, cunt, cut
Clit, clot, slit, slot, slut, shun, shit
Lift, beat, meat, milk, smoke, choke
Fake, fate, eat, egg, ovum, drown
Bone, stone, tongue, ova, vulva, moan
Chromosome, blonde, bomb, scum, slim
Slime, slide, knife, glide, inside
Formaldehyde, deride, debride, collide, divide
Ride, rid, red, bleed, head, blood, incubus
Nimbus, succubus, bust, breast, blast, blister
Pus, pussy, rust, ring, sting, string
Stink, pink, blink, blank, cock, black
Rack, break, slake, suck, fake, fuck, take
Snake, shed, bled, Gilead, glory, story
Whore, warden, war, garden, Eden, queen
Green, tree, free, fruit, root, rot, truth, taint
Saint, slut, slave, strip, lip, frigid, fair
Foul, feline, false, famous, fallen, free

It is what it is

Paper   flutters and tears in the gusts
sails like featherless birds   There's a piece of blue sky
on this note   a ball of clay below collects footprints
a hand grasps a phone   tendons shrink
to pull fingers toward a circle of pink palm
an orb in blackened flesh   from a land of desiccated
hope   nineteen bring the fire that pulls the digits
toward the wrist   charred bodies dive toward caskets
or become dust beneath the cushion of air
steel, flesh, ash   all become earth from sky
hurtle past papers shot in graceful arcs and loops
from shattered windows   bodies plunge through columns of smoke
a man   a woman   jump hand-in-hand and fall
their choice to fall together   in grace

East Memphis

In every sorrow there is profit (Proverbs 14:23)

Girls walk together, arm-in-arm
their denim skirts modest and long,
each covered elbow must not seek
the sun.

Small houses circle round the school;
each Sabbath day, they stroll to shul.
Thick hair pulled back erratically,

tendrils escape by noon each day;
a girlfriend tucks them back again.
It's hard to be chaste at sixteen.

They often hold each other's hands,
pretending to avoid the eyes of boys
who wish, but never voice
the dangerous, forbidden words of love.

Men rise to meet the nascent sun.
They don their kippas, clip them down.
Wool tsitsit hang beneath each shirt,

Humash reveals a parashah.
Foreheads enlaced, left toward the heart;
with leather blessed before the knife,

they shokel as the Torah flame
ignites a vast, complete, celestial soul.
They know in faith this is their world.

Each glance direct, each voice assured.
Hashem instructs directly here—
these lives carved by dark-hatted men

who lived and died six hundred years ago.

Each boy will travel far in life, Yeshiva. Israel,
a wife who'll clothe herself in wig or hat,
decreed by ritual and rule.

An iron drape of custom will compel her—
cook the Shabbos meal. Bear children. Remain clean
and calm. Embrace this space you're given,
this, you own.

Leviathan

The act did not begin here in this room. No. It did not
start with this rendition, this hooded man stumbling over cement.
It began instead in an airport in Boston, in a lawyer's precision,
in a president's fear that history would not be with him.
Bones lifted by a shirtfront, the man rises, then lies tilted, neck
arched, his world narrowed to a damp cloth that smells of dead men.
His musk lets go, dripping shamefully beneath the board
to mix with water that erases air. His breath, no breath.
His terror, all terror. Callused hands hold the ropes as he strains,
his heels kick at heaven, tendons snake along each trussed arm.
Outside, twilight falls, a desert darkens, and every belief chokes
on swirls of blood and doctrine in a place beyond a law,
without a name.

Homecoming

At 3am, darkness whispers his name.
In dreams he battles demons for his grief,
and still white fires burn far fields the same.

More pills, blunts, cigarettes, he is ashamed
to medicate the hours, seeking relief
from sodden sheets where darkness calls his name.

Fallujah was his soldiers' Gethsemane;
In Babylon, carnage belied belief.
He knows white fires burn far fields the same.

White roses burst through skin, their molten flame
burned men to ash whose lives were brutal, brief.
Maimed comrades bleeding out shouted his name.

In every glass his face appears restrained
but stitches on his wrists betray his strife.
Tonight darkness descends to howl his name
because white fires burn far fields the same.

Swan Song

Mist smokes in strands across a mountain lake this morning.
Light rises beyond peaks caped with last winter's snowfall.
A woman wakes in a bed far from home.

A thousand miles south, dying cattle trudge through sere grass,
thin skins hang over the piano keys of their ribs. A rancher prepares to sell
at a loss. He gazes at the land his grandfather rode, at the home

where his father was born, at the exposed white band of skin ringing
his finger where a woman once held claim. He thinks of far mountains,
of lakes, of empty whiskey bottles, and impotent, midnight anger. His fists flex

as he nears auction signs staked into his earth. Perhaps the relentless heat
will burn the words to ash. He pulls a safety match from his pocket,
flicks it to flame with a thumbnail. On the edge of mountain water,

a woman waits near the shore, tracks a solitary cygnet as he floats a love cry
across the still expanse. No welcoming echo enfolds him, so he swirls away
into the distant, rising fire of the sun.

For the Women

Once more, rocks wait in stadiums of dust.
Hands press to wounded heads or claw the dust.

The people silence singing, shutter shops.
Razors all stilled, beards draw the Afghan dust;

Red poppies lie destroyed and laughter ends.
The fields fall fallow, raw, returned to dust.

Bearded Pashtuns eye every shadowed street,
Salvage the holy law from boot-stomped dust.

Young soldiers marched away, taking their bombs.
The female teachers' graves merge straw with dust.

Dark rivers freeze below the Khyber Pass.
Come summer, flesh will thaw to mix with dust

Near Peshawar, a sister has transgressed.
Her purple thumb, whipsawn, collects the dust.

An unveiled face once more courts suicide.
And girls, forbidden books, withdraw to dust.

The women all retreat behind burkas.
Each temptress hidden from flawed men of dust.

A man exits a cave above the plains.
His followers, in awe, kneel in the dust.

El Día de los Muertos

"The path back to the living must not be made slippery by tears."
(Mexican proverb)

Marigolds blaze yellow under Oaxacan sun.
Their slender necks stretch above fern foliage.
Stars of this late October hillside, they drape
their riches over the edges of terra cotta
like a beautiful woman lounging naked on a chaise,
 denying the time-bound limits of beauty.

They wear their bodies recklessly, these cempazuchitl,
these flowers of the dead. Soon, an elder's hand
will pluck them from this life, mix their petals
 on the ofrenda, shrouded by the incense of copal,
 the backs of his descendants bent beneath a colder sun.

Subsuming their bright allotment on foreign soil,
the lost children of Mictecacihuatl dream of sugared skulls
and warm hojaldra as they lie under a canopy of snow.
Someday they, too, may return to wreathe the fleshless grin
of this country, the nexus of their souls. La Pelona is filled
but never sated with the bodies of her dead.

IV. Vibrato

Ages

Age I — Black

Bereft of oestrous
night sweat sheets
simulate passion flown

Age II — Gray

An overcast eye
gentles every landscape

Age III — Blue

My mother's veins
river my hands

Age IV — Yellow

Brittle   t e e th
                    c
               r
                    o
                        o
                    k
                    e
               d

          b
       o
              n
          e
       s

curl over
bunioned feet

Age V— Green

Dying is one gift
our children keep

The Rest Home

Here, at the other end of your life
you drift in dreams
and do not know my name.
Today, I am Tom, a brother,
the younger, the favorite.
"Dad, I'm not Tom," I say.
Confusion clouds your once bright eyes
and silence numbs your tongue
while fingers fiddle across the air,
sewing cloth I cannot see.
I have never known this man.
He is not who he is.
"What is this place?" he asks again.
What is this place, indeed.

Self-Portrait

There is little risk in painting yourself invisible.
Stripped of old habits, there is talent in capturing
the image of no one.

Another day waits
to be endured, balanced loosely
like a brush held by unremarkable fingers.

Ignore the colors that tempt from the palate.
They eventually assume the deadly brown
of footprints struck in the muck of rain-pelted clay.

Do not count on mirrors, they offer no reflection.
Danger rests in believing the honest blue of the sky.
It will break your heart to presume you can see.

June, Texas, 1993

My father kneels on the St. Augustine,
hands braiding in green and white repair of a torn lawn chair.
His fingers thick, right thumbnail puddled with a blue bruise.
Head tilted, his eyes focus on this morning's work.
A wasp swings its glassy wings beneath the eave
to daub more mud on the coned dome it fashions
which we do not destroy. Its brown husk will remain,
dry and solid, long after my father's return to clay.
And still he kneels, fearless, and weaves.

For Rebecca

Now falls the dark hour of your mother's song.
The scattered ashes fall. How to continue?
Your music drifts, you're in her mind, but gone.

You leave your scent on sheets, pictures you've drawn.
The sky denied, today dawns black, not blue.
Now falls the dark hour of your mother's song.

Your loved ones try to mask their devastation.
The children left behind, the older two
hear music call, you're in their minds, but gone.

A picture from September brings her longing,
a ribboned dress, your violin, your shoe.
Now falls the dark hour of your mother's song.

Dark clouds scud low to brush the shadowed lawn.
Each morning hones a sharper blade of truth.
Dawn's music troubles and reminds you've gone.

Rebecca, glitter, flutter off alone.
The earth offers a space for only you.
Now falls the dark hour of your mother's song.
The music drifts. You're in her mind. You've gone.

You Tell Yourself

House guests do not investigate bags and boxes
stashed in closets while one's host is away.
Your mother taught you this well. No need to meet
past lovers through letters not addressed to you.

There are reasons ghosts lie stacked and folded
in hollows, away from the glow of stars.
You tell yourself you do not want to learn new lessons,
so closets are out, backs of cupboards unfair game.

Ignore the queasy allure, that itch to crawl
inside and embrace another's secrets, to search
for the exact scrap that maps his past and tells you
what it is that makes a riddle of his smile.

Old words and photos stacked beyond the light wait
like baited hooks. Compelling, perhaps even forgotten
by your host, they tempt you in the quiet
of this solitary day. Remind yourself there are rules:

Polite guests stick to perusing bookshelves and refrigerators.
Perhaps the carpet needs attention. Sharpen his knives,
or just sit while his old dog licks your toes and explore
the sunlight that leaks lemony through the patio screen.

Release

Here, the silence in the wide hall complicates your nights.
You wake, search rooms for sounds of need.
Here, now, the absence of the shush of rubber wheels on tile,
the metal chair cradling the birdlike body, her ethereal eyes.
Here, the empty bed, its metal rail, its buttons, a bell.
perfume gone bronze in its bottle, her hairbrush, her paintings.
Here, the unspeakable lightness of grief.

Midnight, 1960

The lamp's yellow halo
paints my mother's dark curls.
Smoke swirls around her face
as she reads, a tea pot in its cozy,
rose-painted cup and saucer near.
Pall Mall butts lie discarded
in the ashtray, tipped with Avon's
latest red. Settled in the book,
she raises delicate fingers
to her pink tongue, dabs a sliver
of tobacco from its tip. Never
taking her eyes from the pages
cradled in her lap, she lives
another life. My father
snores, rooms away, unaware
of the change taking place
in the cooling, midnight air.

Legacy

—For Addie

The river runs as the boatman rests, arms slick
with the sweat of his toil. Just past mid-stream,
we bathe ourselves in poetry, lace our bones
into corsets of poems, slide the silk wrappings of words
over our shoulders to cushion this coming of night.
Today, an infant girl swims from her mother's womb
toward a milky breast. In the same hour, twenty children
sweep to the farther shore. No time to drop smooth pebbles
as they passed, their flute-like voices call over vast distance.
Darkness waits always just beyond the fire. This is the truth
I would keep from you. At sundown, night tangles its fingers
in auburn leaves that flutter through San Marcos' streets.
A red-haired baby sleeps; earth's breath strokes a perfect cheek;
a poem's music flicks the first ripples of language that heals,
that cries, that lives. This choice, to sing with the tongue
and the teeth, the sibilant s, the slender skin of mother sound
wrapped around your tender skull, *I love you* spoken
just before a pink-lipped kiss: this ferocious love is the alpha,
the omega. Patient Charon, eyes a flamed-tipped blue,
poles his bark to shore, shoulder brushing silver willows.
We wait to board. Because you have come, child of our child,
we know he comes for us. Pens poised, we write our truths
for the living on multi-hued paper, tie strings of meaning
to your tiny fingers; will you these pages when we pass.
Flesh coats unbutton in the slow dance of unbecoming.
We are shades, backlit by copper tipped waves. We step
from these bodies, our imperfect shields, and drape them at last
on the pyre. Words weave in patterns, the marks of goodbye,
then rise with our smoke to the moon wounded sky.

Counting

Three hundred and sixty-five twice gone.
I want to talk to you again, help you fix a fan,
trim a hedge, pound a nail, paint a bedroom yellow.
We sat numb, exhausted, inarticulate
while those dark faces that surrounded you
in the dying turned, tested, timed your breaths,
I picture practical watches; thick soled shoes, and drops
of Morphine, the gentle hospice man who lovingly cleared
the rattle from your throat eased your suffering
while we cringed outside the door, afraid of the tube.

Seven hundred thirty days.
I can't remember, was it a Monday? Thursday?
The pool needs patching, the ceiling, too.
Your voice remains a constant in my inner ear.
I miss your stories. Gato Slindy, the baseball game, the ex-lax.
The neighbor tossing filthy washwater
from her window calling, "for the birds."
Some say the forgetting begins before the first hour
recedes, as colors bleed to gray, one by one
until there are none but shades of shadow
left to trouble the air. I want to show you
the fence I painted, learn to hang a fan with you.

Two autumns, two springs.
I want to explain how rain shreds the sky
in silver filaments less and less now—
How last winter, hail bulleted the pool water
and startled the cats from their slumber.
Pete's muzzle is grizzled, his bark tosses flute-like
against the morning air to frighten no one. I am older.
The light seems changed, and winter blows warmer
as city buses' brakes shrill beside the house
to trouble my sleep.

I recall your nose, how prominent and Roman
at the end; that thin, clarified line at the finish,
how your earlobes curled to shamrocks, so soft
beneath my fingertips, still warm.

V. Intermezzo

Crossroads

I passed Iniquity a long ways back. There was only one bar with a Shiner sign blinking brokenly through the dust-flecked window and a one-pump gas station with a soaring red horse painted on the bathroom door. A violet-tinted old lady in ankle-rolled hose sat on a braided lawn chair beside a wicker basket full of turnip greens at the crossroads. Robert Johnson wasn't there at all.

Empires Fall

She's a loaded gun fingers flexing on the trigger she's the 3 am gritty-eyed one last line before oblivion turning and turning in the darkness knotting of sweat-sogged sheets she's a winding shroud of whiskey that coats the breath she's the paisley smoke that halos auburn hair she's teeth that grind an empty room a burning fuse and sweeping slants of black tracks down pale skin she's a desiccated womb a silhouette a sway before a broken mirror she's bloodmist and milky bone she's a fire sparked its flickering blue notes singing deep beneath the temples she's a trajectory complete she's the vulture winging overhead the string of broken pediments. The aftermath, a ringing, meets the day

Catch Trap

She's worked in the business since she was thirteen when daddy inserted his blood-crusted key. Years later, as paint peels, the woof and warp cants, he leaves her his ashes to spread on the clay. She won't leave the counter; it's all Marlee knows. When men stop to pay her, she's easy with smiles. She's served bankers, bus drivers, and one or two bums. Night watchmen occasionally toss her some cash after filling their tanks, but they all disappear. Handprint smudged doors turn the few passers-by into silent cartoons Marlee watches all day. She hawks Parliaments, hot dogs, and ice-clustered Cokes, but her loyalty, even on discount, won't sell. Posted signs ask the rough men to please wipe their feet, but frayed edges soon crumple, ink fades in the sun. Mud clotted work boots leave streaks down the aisles like striped bruises she hides under uniform sleeves. After midnight she padlocks the entryway doors, escapes to dark barrooms, then whiskey-fueled sleep. In her dreams there's a bed of red feathers and dew, bejeweled mosses drape grottos, frame purple lagoons. She climbs a steep cliff toward the blue chenille sky where trapezes sway chained to foam-headed clouds. It's a space where a father's fists can't beat a child, and hope never wings from a punch-swollen eye. She alters her grip on the links as she swings between bars sloughing silver and bits of fool's gold. Gaining speed, Marlee leaps from one man to the next, terrified of the space in between.

For the Lost Boys

A milky-eyed dog yips in dreams. Gray muzzle, matted hair, a limp his medal of heroic dog battles with buses and postman shoes. A tattered tail batons a medley of insect song on a shotgun house's back porch. A brave dog, he fought to acquire important dog things: squirrel tartare, whisker of cat, abundant fornication; his boy's gentle hand only a wag away. Things happen to young black boys at the bottom of this place. An education stands no shield when drunken blood sport bullets by with the flash of a gang sign, a chain's sharp edges, and a singing Mac10 to obliterate a face. Banded black arms strain against the pull of brass handles bolted into wood. A mother's legs give way, and she must be carried to her chair. The raw earth beneath the mourners' feet is covered with a cape of green. The future of a family is buried in Reverend Gray's churchyard as an old dog waits at home. Blind, the dog points his nose to the crowd shuffling into the empty house, searching for the scent of his boy who will never become a man.

La Luz de la Salida

Spring roses bloom beyond the bedroom window; their canes stretch each petaled head toward a waking April sun. Inside, the room lies shadowed, thick with sudden silence.

Sitting on her bed, the old woman bends forward, stretches across the expanse to touch her husband's face. Her fingertips stroke his delicate arm, its paper thin skin still precious, still warm.

Light from the hallway sheens an oil cross painted on the old man's forehead. The weary priest kisses his beads, rises from his knees, and walks toward the open window to watch for morning.

A spark darts and weaves through the death-disturbed air, stops to hover above the priest's sleep-tousled hair. It flames and it flickers, then shoots past the roses in spangles of fire toward the light, just ahead.

The Cost

A black bear claims these woods. Slovenly and drunk, his paws swipe unthinking at his cubs, a rictus of a smile flashes teeth mossy with scum. On Friday nights, he knocks them about the mazzards as bitter ribbons of whiskey fumes flow from his open maw. The cubs know better than to walk inside his shadow, and they've learned to avoid his eyes and conversations about politics, mothers, or wages. Almost big enough to light out, they will never be grown. They stand at the edge of their lives and cast stones at the future, but gravity pulls them down before they can fly. Their lean skins hang over bones like clownish coats, and they play pranks on other cubs that often result in injury. Their mother rides the rodeo circuit, tangling with half-crazy cowboys for twenty dollars a throw while an old pipe organ plays jarring, tired tunes for the rowdy crowds. Even in chains, her teeth shaved down to useless nubs and her claws removed, she never, ever wants to go home.

Lex Talionis

In the City of Angels, you lean in shadowed entryways, the smell of piss and taco stand grease wafting past your face. Traffic slides by as you search for a special woman, the secret of her existence hidden deep inside each whore's bitch-sharp eyes.

You've learned to hustle a special cut of meat down here on the tenderloin. You go with one of them; his back offers bright stripes of color to carrion eaters like you, so you prepare, wear the hood, crack the whip.

The old man's face haunts your waking hours. The bubbling spittle that flecked his lips, the calloused hand that became one with the whip, and the smell like rotted meat that blew from his open shirtfront with each swing:

"Gotta watch that sinnin' Bird-boy. Might be more damnation in your soul than I can fix with this striper. Sweet salvation rests in prayer and repentance. There's virtue in sufferin', blackbird. Tears are for sissies."

In dreams, you see the dark hand that grabbed at his crotch, hips pumping in a frenzied dance at your eye level. You see black half-moons under yellow fingernails. "This here root made you, and I damn sure can take you out."

He'd tie your mouth shut, your spit freeing the taste of his sweat on the kerchief, your ears tingling with the music of the whip down your spine, the grunts of pleasure erupting from his throat as your little boy skin split in ribbons across your back.

You can't remember when it wasn't so, the Root man swinging pig leather that sang in measured meter while your thin wrists, tied with gut, hung from the bedposts. Before the fire, you focused on your thickening strength as you ate anything you could steal from the kitchen before the nights when your back swayed to the music of the whip and blood ran down the edge of the ruined mattress.

Tonight you lie on a foreign mattress far from the Piney woods. The sour tang of Wild Turkey slides across your lips as you try over and over to master this dialectic he offered in return for your soul.

After you flew you wondered about the woman who twinned with the Root man to deposit you there. He'd get shitty-ass drunk, point west, and mumble "Good riddance to a bad whore." Where is the mother who should have stopped the thick leather from tearing your childhood from you, leaving you to bleed with a bible as schooling and vengeance the Root man's only release?

In a rented room off a boulevard a thousand miles west, you still hear him some nights, shouting from the log-walled living room, the humidity clawing at the rips in the screens, bugs sizzling and popping under the flames, the kerosene fire licking at his tethered feet as you ran through the Mississippi pines, your legs slippery with yellow ooze. Cold showers can't quench the heat of his screams burning into your head:

"Think you bested me? I'll never let you be. You ain't never been nothin' to no one. You motherless bastard. I'll come after you. One way or other, you ain't never gonna be free."

The real hunt begins tonight, after the final burning swallow of bourbon. You'll search for her through the darkness and the neon. A leather strop waits coiled and ready in a pocket for a woman who ran west and left nothing but a bible and hellfire behind.

Imago

The woman slides aside the curtain. Her face peeks out in silhouette to take in all the perfect little hands holding nets. Bodies bounce and hands swoop toward wings struck with yellow, black, brown, orange, white. She hears laughter from children who chase monarchs across the milkweed pasture beyond the tumble-down fence. Their mothers have warned them not to risk nearing the shuttered house.

Day and night reflect in her black eyes. She remains secluded in shadow, her chest barely moving in, out. Arms flutter like broken birds at her sides. Spiders weave webs in the chiaroscuro of her hair as daylight slivers stab the air and dust motes slant, frozen in mid-flight. She tugs the curtain closed and makes her dragging way downstairs to key open the basement locks and recede from the morning that beckons beyond the drapes.

She smiles at what waits below.

Down here there is rope work and wood, hanging lights fashioned for warmth. A fire in the grate exhales the scent of apple smoke mixed with chloroform. Pulling a chair close behind her, she sets aside her cane and reaches up to weigh a giant pupa in her palms as it hangs clustered with its mates, fantastic table grapes depended from a trellis on the ceiling. Beyond the trellis, scattered on worktables, are test tubes and curling papers, aquariums filled with eggs and zebra-yellow caterpillars clinging to thin-veined leaf stalks; there are glass beakers, dusty books filled with chimeras and schemes.

With a practiced tug, a cocoon falls like a jade vase into her arms. She slides it between her knees, balances the tip against the floor. The silver blade clamped between her hands, she knives a slit to vent the carapace, then handles the chrysalis like a lover, running her palms down its delicate, chartreuse shoulders. Carefully, she lays the pupa on its side near the warm fire.

Squatting, she studies her creation, stares into the slit she has fashioned. Forehead damp, her hands squirm, itching to wrench it open. She leans back onto the chair, every muscle tense, and waits for a sign, a movement. Perhaps a magnificent wing will unfurl to flutter and dry in the smoke-scented air. Perhaps she will climb aboard and take to the sky at last. But as every time before, only her breathing breaks the stillness.

Each day, her house peels in flakes that waft over far green hills. Bit by bit, spongy wood and mortar decay to expose the starter fabric of earth and sky. Family grave markers fallen onto the gravel track outside. She cannot fly away from the image of children with fine hands and faces, the laughter she has never shared.

She lifts her eyes toward the failing fire. A space on the trellis is free. She tethers herself with a necklace of rope, imagines a woman with butterfly's wings.

Happy Hour

Before they'll unlock the steel-lattice door, my keys, watch, pin, and wallet must be tossed into a numbered Zip Loc bag. "Sorry, no chocolate bar. No strings, or shoes with laces, no cell phone, no pens. One hour to visit." The door swings shut; the air flags, sluggish. Walls painted undersea green curl like waves around me. I smell vomit as I enter the visitor's room to pull out a stool next to you.

Your words tumble like a jumbled puzzle: "I went to the Cowboy's game with Jerry Jones last night. Did you bring my chocolate? I had lunch at The Grange in Denver with my mother. She wore a butter yellow dress with black heels. The skirt buzzed around her legs when she slid from the booth. She told me when he shot himself, my father's flesh swelled fishbelly blue."

This locked ward is not the oblivion you sought. Each thought a slippery trickster, a shapeshifter. I tell you Jerry Jones is a newspaper picture, The Grange too far from Dallas for a meal with mom; your dad still shoots red squirrels with his .22, and I'm sorry, but they took your chocolate. Your focus fades; thoughts of contraband candy bars disappear.

As I collect my watch and keys beyond the bolts, I picture the bottle of Ativan stirred into a sweating glass of whiskey on the loneliest night of your life while your husband, bags packed, asleep in the next room, bends to kiss his reflection in a shimmering dream pool, thin arms locked in perpetual self-embrace.

Rialto's al Fresco

A woman sits bent over a table as the breeze troubles her hair. A buff envelope lies torn in half on the white cloth. Contents read then crushed, the pages roll off the edge to land amid busy city shoes. Polished nails tick against a wine glass, soft fingers brush imaginary crumbs from her lap, comb through hair, tap the table. Her diamond sparkles, a fairy wing throwing rainbows into her eyes. Hand resting on the black wrought iron rail, she stares at her wedding band, slides it from her finger, drops it beyond the ironwork to the pavement. She cannot seem to place the sky. Sunlight breaks in shards through cumulous; a ray chases the white, white paper scratched with black words as it's kicked to the curb. She sits, sips cabernet, bows her head. Silver sounds of kitchen work are mummified behind the brick facade. Burdened tugs scud the muddy river. Gulls hover above, dive for crumbs. Tomorrow, the delta will flood. Windows paint her profile as she turns to catch laughter that escapes from the bar inside as a waiter backs through the doors and asks, "Ma'am, will there be anything more?" "No," she says, "I'm finished. Nothing for me."

Off the Beaten Path

Father Unick makes love to Dick's elegy from the stone pulpit. Prayers for the dead man are decanted like sacrificial wine. We four, three exes and one current, perch quietly, past beatings undetected, broken bones healed, elation unnoticed by the well-dressed mourners. For better or worse, we gaze through Unick, having exhausted our year-long discussion of the power of latent anger, the solutions we could have chosen. A heady idea, these choices one can make.

We could have been pulp. Buried. Compost. Maybe there in that wood. Instead, the bastard's life was over before he could throw another punch. The arrow exploded skin. Eve's always been a fine shot, and Sally and Dick's final hunting trip a brilliant strategy. Flaps of bloody belly hung through Dick's torn camo. Birds startled as the weapon whistled its Darwinian intent through air followed closely by odd, woman-sounding whoops that echoed over the deserted hunting ground. Dick toppled to the loess, a goon unfit for survival. Drool wet his chins as a great, mortal roar beat the blood-misted air.

Ex-wives and widow, we congregate. Diddle our rosaries. Spit-shine the twenty-third psalm through Altoid-scented breath. Afterward, other people's tongues move thickly with, "terrible accident." and "Yes, just awful." Our Oakley's shade glances that compare old bruises. Practiced deceit directs our muscles in bodies freed of torment by Eve's deeply planted barb. We pat people's hands, wipe away tears.

Later, as one, we empty Dick's urn over the waterside cliff. Back at the church, Father Unick counts Dick's money— his lucrative cameo concluded. Sally, Dick's last punching bag, has access to the accounts. We share a final chance to fondle, sift through Dick's ashes for bits of bone and toss them into the sea. Broken pieces of charred fist sink to lie on beds of sand. Our smooth worry stones are cast after them. Stepping over old scars on the path, we lock arms and head toward a smoky single malt.

Manhattan, Sunday Morning

Heracles tumbles over the wave of a tugboat. His board, strung to an ankle tattooed with an arrow, bobs behind. Waxed and glimmering, an "S" necked swan adorns its surface, the bird's cupped wings shadow a raven-haired woman, as yellowed claws pierce each breast. Her mouth is a slash of red. Stenciled beneath the picture are the words RAD DAD.

Dropping his massive head, Heracles gives up his quest for the perfect wave, suspecting his coordinates are off once again, and pulls his powerful arms against the Hudson's currents to light out across a Jersey garbage barge's wake. White serpent curls unfurl behind as he aims his strokes toward the gypsy cab parked on the wharf above where Pandora waits, driver's cap tilted, skirted knees spread wide beneath the wheel to catch the errant summer breezes.

The New York Review splayed on her lap, Pandora scours the personals. A pink acrylic nail trails the columns for a message from her maker: "P: Hope is alive. Come home. Z," but all she sees is a winter rental in Troy: 3 BR, 2 BA, breathtaking views, sand, surf, wine dark sea, parking—perfect for her upcoming getaway from this muscle-bound fool. She lights an Eve and sighs out the smoke as Heracles drips into the passenger seat, wiping bloody palms pierced by zebra mussels against the cloth triangle between his thighs.

Pandora turns the key, flips the cab into drive, and scans the face of the sky through the filmy windshield, searching for a thunderbolt, the lost taste of Ambrosia teasing her tongue. She tosses Heracles a dirty towel as Icarus, eyelids painted candy-apple green, soars past the glass and shoots them the bird. His delicate feet drag against the blue as twined wings of eagle feather, reed, and wax angle his young shoulders through a break between his father and the incandescent sun.

Almonds

I pour your espresso as though you are a guest, slide the lemon twist to spread its oil along the rim of the delicate bone cup, use the best china for your requisite yogurt and dates.

"Won't you eat?" you ask me, glancing at the singular place setting.

"I ate before the light." I say. Your eyebrow climbs your forehead, suggesting my approach to breakfast, along with the hundred other errors I make daily, is an oddity. We are wondrous in our formality these mornings.

Your hand fondles your bare head and rests there for a moment. I almost laugh, then resist the urge. A blind habit, your palm always looks like a nightcap you've forgotten to remove. When you were twenty-five and I fourteen, your sable hair gleamed under the Iranian desert sun and smelled of anise.

I do not laugh; you hate to look absurd.

French doors open to the chill September day, I carry your tray to the balcony. A faint scent of almonds trails from your cup as the breeze ruffles the Belgian lace cloth spread over the table. I set your meal in front of you. A hint of perfume lifts from your skin when I stoop near your cheek; its Asian spice is not mine. I back away, almost knocking over the demitasse, then recover myself.

Your lips pressed into a thin white line, you shake your head and look down as if I am a mongrel dog who has pissed the Tabriz and say, "Your toenail polish is chipped."

The pages of the newspaper paper rustle over your belly as you clear your throat of me. I stand with my back turned and gaze five floors down to the gypsy world of the Saturday market two blocks away, its chatter of women in their rainbow of shawls and sensible shoes floats lightly on the air. They waddle through the colorful tents and stalls poised at the edge of the Black Sea bargaining for turnips and greens in a language I will never understand. An airport taxi pulls to into a space just outside the entry doors below.

I know you plan to be gone again tonight when you say "My tan suit is at the cleaners. Please pick it up before five." I think of brown leather bags packed with cash and hidden in the extra room.

As you take the first sip, my vision constricts as if I am sighting through a lens this moment, this place. Here on this terrace it is just you and me and the potted date palm we smuggled from Iran so long ago. Its knife-like leaves flutter shadows across the rictus of your astonished face. I turn my back on you, walk through the apartment to collect my bags. My imperfect feet and I have a flight to catch and connections we must not miss.

VI. Adagio

Two Rooms

Jigsaw men smoke behind cinder block walls,
assemble the pieces of people they've been.
Second-hand voices seep under the door
of the coffee-cup room severing "Al" from "Anon"
—Pain extended from pain embraced.

On this side, new converts speak hushed or hurried,
wet-eyed, or wrung dry. Blank lives assume form
with each word offered here, like "he did" and "he said"
or "I told him to go..."

...While the "he" men all speak of the people they've been.

The newly birthed "nons" of us pay off our debt,
count each hour we focus on "me," "I," not "*he.*"
Each survivor exposes a skin pink with scars.
Filtered he-air intrudes as we salve open wounds.

"He said," Kleenex weeps...
"He did," Lost begins...

...While the men in the next room chant Me, Me, Me, Me!

We women work puzzles, avoid those with eyes
while the jigsaw men talk of the people they've been.

Joani Reese

Divestiture

Today the list seems endless,
trinkets I can give away.
A wedding ring, a house,
a grand piano, clothes in disarray.

Your culinary library can stay—
I'll choose a book or two.
The mitre saw? The Philip's head?
Take them. I'll even leave the screws.

You say perhaps I'll reconsider
—promise me you'll change your ways.
It's much too late to supplicate—
the Volvo goes; Suburban stays.

The vodka bottles tempt you, don't they?
Stashed behind your office drapes.
Afraid I'll pack them? Wrong, my friend,
I only want a clean escape.

I'll take the bonds, the 401's
to raise our sons—your gun remains.
Perhaps you'll have the decency
to use it and blow out your brains

No, don't accuse. I'll be in touch,
I can't say how and won't say when.
It's really just become too much.
Divest me, dear. Begin again.

Final Note #1

I took
the Phillips head.
You never knew how to
use it anyway.   I left the
children.

Final Note #2

I left
the Phillips head.
Your tongue's thick with whiskey.
Go screw someone more galvanized
than me.

Ghosts

Your phone has been disconnected
yet somehow you manage to call them
from your denouement in Florida.
You need someone to cry to,

your unending troubles barb
into the fabric of their thin, boy-man
skin. They cling for days afterward
to the meaning behind your call,

search for their own reflections
in the shining fish hooks of your words.
They shovel through the shit and stink, hoping
to claim the man they imagine still hovers

beneath the mire. Your second wife
has tossed you out. Tired of 8 am toasts,
she flings you and your empty pockets to the dirt
outside and slams the door, pours herself

a celebratory flute of champagne,
leaves you with nothing but a hollow ringing
in your skull, a used car, and a passport sporting
a blurred photograph with its rictus of a smile.

I wonder if your bottom lip still aches
where I punched you twenty years ago
in the blackest of nights when you tore
at my nightgown with your Miller Lite

hands, the boys still babies, dreaming down
the dusky hallway, drunken monsters hovering
above their heads. Even then they knew
no one would ever save them.

2008, What I Wanted

I wanted it to be 2007, before my husband lost
his white collar and our nest egg broke its shell against
the blind windows of Wall Street. I wanted not to feel
the clench in my guts every time the bills came due.
I wanted to believe my son, almost grown, would head
to college and enjoy the life my parents provided me.
It is 2011. My son works overnights. Mornings at seven,
I hear him climb the stairs toward his day's rest.
If I am quick, I may catch a trace of his boy's smile,
testing itself against an older, stranger's face.

8 am

This is the story of how you lean in the doorway,
cheek bones etched with turquoise crayon.
Lines snake across your forehead; crude arrows
slide over the knobs of your shoulders.

You have prepared for war while I slept
through the small hours of this summer night.
You've protected your brain with a striped hat,

fur-lined earflaps and brim. Pom-pom ties sway
across your hollow chest. I smell smoke
on your breath, stale Budweiser on your clothes.

Your sleeveless t-shirt is the same faded black
you wore yesterday. Clavicles rise in sharp angles
beneath night-white skin.

I know you've been gone again and are still traveling
away from me. Your lips peel and flake, arms hang
at your waist: thin, blue-veined, sad.

This is the story of how I want to brush the dust
from the clocks, lift the heavy curtains from your eyes.
I picture the piping voice and gleaming face

of a three year old boy gazing up at me
and grinning a freckled grin, showing me
his sandbox castle with its protective moat.

This is the story that says I want to close
the bedroom door, escape from your ashen
presence to what might have been. But instead,

I smile from the distance of my chair,
nod my head when you pause for a moment

between flights of ideas. I want to know

what to do, tell you what pill to take, what pill
not to take, what thought to think, what fears
to shed, what book to read, what life to live,

how to be happy,
but I don't know any of this.
This is the story of what I long to do

but do not do. I want to gentle your tired
face, safe against my body, stroke
your matted hair, feed your disappearing flesh

and promise you all will be well. I want to repair
the broken places say I'm sorry beg forgiveness
for whatever this is I do not understand. Instead,

years of ghost words clot the air between us,
edges sharp as razors slicing veins,
and we cannot stumble through them

without blood. So you turn away, and I watch
you retreat up the stairs, to your war paint,
your empty bottles, your anger,

and I say nothing, but as I hear your tread
fade up the stairway, I pray that when you do finally
find sleep, you'll wake again to give us both another chance

to unearth the courage to speak of love,
of loss. But today, this frail glimmer
beneath silence and sorrow must suffice.

Night Chorus

Achieving Sobriety

After he wandered from the house,
baby Cory scattered himself like bread
on the winter waters of Lake Mendota.
We carried him home, diaper dripping, lips blue.
Mary, still sotted, pulled on ashen clothes.
She rocks at the window most days, watches for birds.

Topos

I have spent five years preparing to leave this city,
a flat, dry place of endless roofs that layers its citizens
in safety from the great unwashed, those others
with bat-shaped eyes who hover on the edges
just below them—those who have fallen from the ceilings.
I am falling, too, plummeting from the middle class.
I do not know where I will land. The roadway beyond
the berm, boasting zebra grass and sage, embraces
the steel machines that percuss beyond my bolted door.
Pity the expense of it all, the cost of repair, these rooms
requiring constant care. I am, at last, the empty bottle,
green glass streaked by runnels that mark the end
of a vessel's use, cork cracked. I arm myself
with the hammer and claw, nail loose fence boards
in plumbed relief, paint eight years of stain away.
A cry is muffled in a sunrise kitchen. The air fogs,
clotted with fumes, words unspoken. A grackle swings
its light-touched wings beyond the panes that belong to me
only a little longer. The bird's ebony eyes shine as it beaks
upward into a finch-fled Texas sky. Words are useless,
so I rip the newspaper to bits. Its language dead, stripped
of meaning, pages catch the drips from the roller, the drops
from the brush. Tilting on a topography too weak to bear
my weight, I color the spaces neutral to please an unknown palate,
then press the sign that begs for release mid-point into the edged
and polished lawn. I wonder why the clay won't cleave
from south to north and take me, skidding, home.

Punch Lines

I'd hoped to have landed now,
bruised, but intact, a cigarette
burning the clench from my chest,
but I'm spinning in treetops
through fist-broken air. He
shouldn't have cut me; he loves
me, he claims, as the crust
of his spittle dries tight on my face.
The screen door is locked; maybe
he'll wake up soon. I sway
on the porch swing and sing
in my blood to the moon.

For a Wounded Boy

Each evening an elephant bursts through the door to play hide and seek with the man who haunts this house. Boy pretends he's not here, never welcomes the brute, relies solely on silence, hopes that he'll disappear.

At cocktail hour, stinking piles dapple the den. Boy's mother shovels them up come morning. As she toils, she hides found objects: empty prescription bottles, glasses dregged with wine, bruises. She pulls shame from pockets, tosses it into the brackish air.

By ten, Boy has furnished a "no-big-deal" room he's built inside his head; a spot cleansed of whiskey, where elephants and men are punished for trampling family dinners, birthday parties, Christmas gifts.

At thirteen, wishes for one normal day consume Boy's hours. The elephant disappears each morning-after, but the man soon regroups, calls the beast back each night saying, *come on in, only one, just one more, dear….*

As he grows, Boy will learn to avoid thrusting tusks, flee from leathery skin and the dung-heap that's home— And the truth? It's unspeakable. Never admit to the guilt, just stare through it with unfocused eyes.

At eighteen, thoughts will dare him to speed the next curve, leap unseeing from unexplored cliffs — fall or fly. He'll have learned to shun joy with its dangerous touch and to puncture each smile with a cynical thrust.

As a man, Boy will think that he's not good enough, stuff his closets with needs that have never been met by the vague, undependable men of his world. And someday, when his life becomes too much to bear, he will open the door to the beast that lived here.

Father

At the other end of your life
you hand me a faded photograph of a young boy
wearing a first new coat —

a third son's shy smile peeks out
from beneath an older brother's discarded cap.
Here, too, is your own father not yet vanished

into a bottle of brandy, no sound of glass shattering
against the metal can outside your open window at midnight.
Here, in this picture, a favorite brother is not yet dead,

grief waits to be introduced; a war is yet to be fought,
a life to be lived. I am not yet here, either.
Here, washed in sepia, is the younger face of one

who never concedes to roots sprung from poverty,
or speaks ill of a mother who tithed to the Jesus of Catholicism
over the rumblings of her children's empty bellies.

Here, too, blow the bitter winters of Madison,
deep hunger leading you over ice-bound lanes to find work,
—never a pause to warm your hands at the fire,

no time to read of Odysseus, Hector, Eros, only a shadow
of that other, Pluto, of the dead. Here, alone,
this childhood that was yours.

We Sit Together Friday Evening

...and Elizabeth says she knows this to be true:
Each step defines patterns on the earth below my feet
in a lonely dance of circular footprints that spiral, reverse,
edge forward, drop back, until the beginning becomes the end.

She is aware that I don the cloak of a smile each evening,
its fiber thinned to a ghost that floats across each room.
Elizabeth counsels patience, says this is the path I chose.
Still, she knows one sip will not diminish my thirst.

She is intimate with the literature of my existence,
dry habits that hold these eyes to each familiar page.
That there is no rising action from which I cannot anticipate
a fall, that there is no more, no less, than this hour, this day.

On a morning when I have settled, opened my book to a page
where I thought my place had been, the journey is new.
A stranger offers secrets, treasure, undeclared gold that fills
the empty pockets of my day, and soon, I begin the leaving.

I wrap my hope in precious cloth and hide it. Terrified,
I want, and then despair, that my breath might slow again
to a static rhythm, that the blunt thrust of this wandering heart
will surrender to the dimensions of its cage.

I ask Elizabeth if she thinks this love I've found
may be a chapter that remains to be written.
Elizabeth tells me she does not know the answer,
but she offers a pen, a blank page. We begin.

VI. Coda

Dream

—For Annie
I see my mother dancing,
damp skin aglow, bare feet
sculpting circles
in the moonlight silvered sand.

Tanagers wing their evening way
across the Puerto Rican sky.
My mother laughs; a Heron lifts
its head, majestic in his stilt-legged

pose, alert, but unafraid
of Mami's joy. Her body ripples
like a breeze as orchid petals
droop with bees. Her striped

skirt twirls around her thighs.
My father follows
with his eyes her daring,
dizzy, death-defying dance.

Soft mangoes fill a cloth
tossed down, as yellow
as the island moon. We eat
the slices hungrily; their juice

runs warm over our chins.
My Mami's cheeks flush pink,
to rose, hibiscus tucked
behind an ear; her hair curls

from the sea born air, as blue-black
as the beachward waves. She bends
to grab my father's hand, then pulls him
from the cooling sand, to dance.

Counting Coup

Cast your pearly line into space,
watch it trace circles as it soars
toward the milk-water sky.
You focus, intent on hooking
the seasons that have flown
without notice in these years
of strife. Three shining hooks
dangle, they tangle with fragments
of dream scenes where autumns
and springs leave no trace.
They mingle with months
you have tried to forget,
then brush past those days
that you wish you had kept.
A March floats above you,
then scares and escapes.
A whole year drifts by
in a flutter of rage. The winter
your father succumbed
you were numb, but you reach
out to touch as he drifts on the wind,
a butterfly wing frozen hard
to his gray laden head.
Entangled in April, last June
tries to break from the line
but is snagged by a hook
through its iridized wing.
You reel in frayed pieces of time
then release them to waver and swing
as the filament sings over earth
with a raggedy lay. They tumble
around you and fill the far hills,
some jagged, some small
as those pain damping pills
that you swallow to keep

every sadness at bay.
Some months sidle closer
and brush past your lips,
flayed puzzles your memory
can never repair. The snared
snippets flounder and ground
while still others, disturbed,
sink beyond a horizon of flames.
Serene Aprils twirl over gorse
as it wavers near other days
tossed in the moss cluttered stream.
So pack up your rod, stand,
and shoulder your basket,
its fern fronds lie dampened
but empty of yield. The sun fails
behind you, one path forks
toward memory. You turn
from the past as you tamp down
desire for those years you can never
recoup nor reclaim.

Autumn, 2001

We always believed that spring would come;
believed that summer would flower again,
ill-prepared for this season of drought.

The Angel-Wing mounds in finished growth.
Petals drop over each berm.
Red cherries ripen under an Indian sun.

Apples firm for picking, their juice runs tart, cool
over our tongues. Seed rests in fallen fruit to spread
what is possible beneath this always uncertain earth.

We crate the remains of this final season;
wrap roots pulled from furrows in yesterday's news;
avert our eyes from its pictures of death.

We shoulder the leavings, our faces bleed ash—
—The end of believing begins.

Black and White

That little detail
in an old photograph,
seemingly insignificant—
that broken toy
on the ground,
a knowing daughter
frowns at her mother,
a fisted hand,
a missing earring,
that reckless weather
in a married lover's gaze.
Each arrests our attention
out of all importance
to its ostensible place
in the composition
of things —That element
unveils a secret
with unintended power,
the unexpected
that makes us wonder
why it is we cannot
look away. The unseen door
through which sorrow saunters
—An uninvited guest
we end up talking to
all evening.

Song of the Other

Nolo timere
—Seamus Heaney

Below the skull of sky, blood leaves a tail.
One-handed, beaten, running, he has failed
To win himself a place beside the fire

A comitatus gathers near the weir.
His loping body cleaves the fetid air.
His steps don't linger; no thing lingers here.

The son of Cain begins his last descent
as strands of seaweed ribbon him and bend
around the jagged trunks of trembling knees.

A storm advances, whirring from the east.
Above his head, two Loons hover and dance,
He slinks back to the womb, a hag's embrace.

All children learn an outcast never wins.
This is no hero: one-armed, ragged, grim.
The swimmer eyes the shore, then dives again.
No poet sings to glorify his end.

Finger Weaving a Voyageur Sash

Twine ribbons: gold, red, emerald, for his eyes
Her furrier trades, her babe a nascent flame.
Her hands keep weaving: Listen to the cries.

This sash will dip for water, tote supplies.
Spread beeswax forms the cup, deft hands the frame.
Twine ribbons: gold, red, emerald, for his eyes

A chevron pattern forms as threads embrace.
Skinned beaver pelts all sold, he paddles home.
Her hands keep weaving: Listen to the cries.

Skilled fingers work, a smile in place denies
approaching screams—perhaps a children's game.
Twine ribbons: gold, red, emerald, for his eyes.

Her focus on each knot fast fingers tie
—not Frenchmen overrun, not bodies maimed.
Her hands keep weaving: Listen to the cries.

Night's air awhirl, the sky shoots fireflies.
Sometimes, she bleeds black arrows in her dreams.
Twine ribbons: gold, red, emerald, for his eyes.

Sad voyageur, death swooped with swift surprise.
Thuds shake the door. A sister screams her name.
Her hands cease weaving: Listen to the cries.

Her lover, bones and ashes where he lies.
and still wild roses star far fields the same.
His sash weaves with the fire's flames that rise
in ribbons: gold, red, emerald, for his eyes.

Disturbance

We linger in the vague, blue hum of another summer. The sudden plummet from the middle dulls our senses and bends our spines closer toward some final ground. Bad decisions, mistakes, hard luck: scar tissue tightens in welts beneath the flesh in wishbone arcs. Deep wounds are always palpable, and blood sport rarely passes without lingering pain. Sparrows dive from the eaves, their love cries filter through the shuttered windows to disturb the white webs we've spun like shrouds around our skulls.

In the night kitchen, we pass in silence as televisions flicker, ghostly in the empty rooms beyond. Each morning breaks its fingers against the granite of our prison; no light enters here. Leaves hang from red oaks, quiver in surrender, a dusty patina settles over each moisture-starved vein. Tendons curl inward on themselves, and still the cleansing rain denies us relief. Yellow weeds choke garden space. There will be weeds next year, too.

We scavenge for crumbs in a world that rejects us, subsist side-by-side in a house of separation, crouch over screens in dark rooms, painting our pain into cartoon frameworks. Our lips recoil from touch. Tongues lie flat and silent through the hours. Necessary words flutter and fall like broken wings from our mouths. Unspoken, words like touch and kiss and love lie trapped between the curving bone while barbed words catch and pull at the air to carve more space between us.

Each blue grows muted within these walls, while outside, a red desert descends. The arm of a flagpole furls no flag, a dog run is undogged, a man buys a country, his currency the face of fear, another buys an arsenal to camouflage his impotence.

A June bug struggles on its back, its legs wave, frantic to climb the ladder of sun. A small boy tilts a magnifying glass over its fumbling trunk, his face passive in the numbness of this mossy age. The bronze carapace cracks and bubbles beneath the glitter that beams from his unforgiving hand. Lips spread in a deaths-head grin, the boy wanders off to seek another game to play.

A windlass creaks over a half empty well, its water wafts a lonely, brackish smell. I finger the pennies singing in my pocket. I close my eyes. I toss them in.

Simulacra

Men drag the last wild woman from her home concealed above a verdigris-tipped sea. A gag secures her mouth; red thread sews closed labial folds. They cuff her hands behind her back and dangle golden keys from chains around their necks. They truck her over the pass to the flatlands, all colors muted green and gray. Pain curls her like a question mark as tamed women bend her bones into the cage where she complies, or dies.

Men blunt her claws, excise her teeth, attack until her mind succumbs. They dress her up; they dress her down. Her face is tattooed with a smile, her womb unlaced, perfectly numbed. She learns to kneel in darkness all her own. Each year evolves into the next. A zealous drab, she sates with sex; she gestates younger, pliant girls, then trains each one to ape a paper doll.

Fifty-Three Seconds

A lone man trudges
      past the grill of my Suburban.
      I hum, tap the wheel,
      impatient with Memphis,
      unsynchronized lights,
      a prisoner of deadlines
      and other-made plans.

      Garrison Keillor reads Yeats over NPR:

      "Had I the heavens' embroidered cloths…"

      A dime-store umbrella bobs above a woman's head
      at the crosswalk; it is freckled
      with bird shit. Her blue uniform hangs loose
      as if stretched by the girth
      of some vanished other. Her face is a closed fist.

      Perhaps I will forgo class today.
      Foucault and Derrida can deconstruct
      the canon without my insight.
      Yes. I'll roll down the window,
      invite her to ride beside me,
      buy her drinks at B.B.'s…

      "…The blue and the dim, and the dark cloths…"

      …learn the names of her grandchildren,
      their ages, tell her I am a writer,
      a failed wife, my Germantown home
      stuffed with tax receipts
      from Amnesty International, Greenpeace,
      brittle letters from long departed lovers…

"...I would spread the cloths under your feet..."

I will hear about her work
on a cleaning crew at one of Beale's tourist traps—
the daily stink of sour juice, vomit,
the hopeless odor of failed fucks
she must sanitize away—
She will speak of her sons,
the daughter who has vanished.

And only, ever, this...

"...but I, being poor, have only my dreams...
        ...Tread softly, because you tread on my dreams."

My eyes focus back on Beale.
The light turns green.

Love Poem

One by silent one, the years cumber our easy steps, add a burden
we can never relinquish. Heartbeats become irregular, faces strange to mirrors.

One day, you look into the face you've loved and find the work of gravity has buried
her laughing, bright-eyed gaze while you dreamed.

Another man would look away, comb the brighter streets for something lost, desperate
to believe that nothing changes, eager to see himself reflected in a younger wom-
an's eyes.

Not you. You cradle that face between your weary hands, finger trace its history
as your own, your lips kiss its ruin from brow to chin, your body finds solace
cupped around her

in the sweet darkness. Take my hand as we circle deeper into evening through
this unfamiliar forest, our careful steps

cushioned by the mosses strewn across the path that leads us far from morning.
We will find the gnarled oak that offers shelter, its autumn leaves struck golden
as they fly.

Luminaria

Night's body submits
to daybreak's caress.
The sun slides over
the shoulders of the hills.
Light enters the valley
and travels in waves,
warming the skin of the river.
Surrender to the senses.
Savor the taste, the touch.
I am the valley, the hills,
the night. You are the heat,
the light of a rising sun.

While the Light Lasts

I.
Pockets stuffed with extra ammo, rifled men deconstruct bodies clinging to steel cables. The trapped link arms on truss ledges: black, brown, white sail into air, leaving red Pollack arcs shooting behind.

II.
Lovers whimper between clenched teeth, then jump, as bullets whiz by overhead. Church women crouch in the uptown direction to bat at passing souls, desperate to save a few, but spirits slip like yellow silk through their fingers and the wind from their leaving floats over the cantilevered arch spanning the blazing river.

III.
Smoke from bodies aflame tongues the strung moon; ashes flake their wings as cardinals litter the sky like liquid roses, their trajectory a drunkards' scribble across the fire-haloed clouds.

IV.
The thump of a falling body startles a cur that scares under the spandrel. Nosing the air, he yips from his hinged jaw, smells his own dog denouement in the gathering atoms of night.

V.
The water's breast is lumpy with meat; painted waves flicker an oily rainbow of expanding heat.

VI.
The fearless dead lie coffined beneath earthen slabs of clay while beyond the water, fires wink out, one by one by one, the light fails, and midnight capes fresh corpses sprouting metal petals from their breasts.

VII.
A neon billboard's words flash a riddle over Times Square no tongue will ever solve. A *New York Times* front page from yesterday tumbles and folds itself around a trembling lamppost.

VIII.

In a hot green room across the river, a red-headed girl flips the pages of a photo album perched atop her nine month belly, a frown on her face. She gazes at photographs collected by those whom she does not yet know have joined the dead. She raises her head and asks the quickening air, *where do people go when they don't come back no more?*

Sand Dollar

Washed ashore, I am the coin
of mermaids in your palm.

Your eyes see only treasure,
not the measure of my end.

The sand moves, sculpted by wind.
Endings clarify, chasten.

Lifted from a suitcase, I am the memory
of sun slashed across a cheekbone,

wind-ruffled sea grass, the curl of foam
that spumes above green waves;

bonfires that sear the night sky,
a kiss from one whose footprints

disappeared beyond the dunes.
I am the arid bone of flowered stars.

Acknowledgements

Many thanks to the following literary magazines and anthologies in which some of these pieces previously appeared:

Versus, Estuary: A Confluence of Art and Poetry, Drifting Down the Lane, Argotist Otherstream Vols. I & II, Thunderclap! National Poetry Month, Festival Writer, Olentangy Review, Thrice Fiction, Blue Fifth Review, Clutching at Straws, JMWW, Pithead Chapel, Stone Highway Review, Big River Poetry Review, the *Glass Coin, Gutter Eloquence Magazine, River Poet's Journal, Blind Oracle Press, Lost in Thought Magazine, Flash Fiction Chronicles, Rigor Mort, A-Minor Magazine, Reprint Poetry, Kitchen Poet, Zocalo Public Square, A Baker's Dozen, Poets on the Great Recession, Eunoia Review, Wilderness House Literary Review, Protest Poems: Writers for Human Rights,* the *Legendary Magazine, Mad Hatter's Review, Nailpolish Stories, Red Fez, Camroc Press Review, Rose & Thorn Journal, Unshod Quills, Connotation Press, Ramshackle Review, Precious Metals: A Poetry Journal, Eclectic Flash, Used Furniture Review, Corium Magazine,* the *Pinch, IBPC, Forces.*

A special thank you and much love to my fellow writers and friends who have unfailingly supported me through both acceptance and rejection: my publisher Jane Carman, Jen Knox, Carol Reid, Sam Rasnake, Bill Yarrow, MaryAnne Kolton, Pamela Ellis Moss, Diana Gingo, Marilyn Kallet, Bud Smith, Heather Fowler, Meg Tuite, spirit-sister Pam Uschuk, and, of course, to my best reader and fan, Patty Reese—long may you wave.

Artist Lisa Cardenas has generously shared her artistic talent with me by lending me her paintings for three gorgeous book covers. I love you, my friend. Thank you.

Joani Reese is the author of two poetry chapbooks: *Final Notes* and *Dead Letters*. *Night Chorus* is her first full length collection. Reese's poetry and fiction have been widely anthologized and featured in both print and online venues. Reese has been poetry editor for *THIS Magazine* and senior poetry editor for *Connotation Press—An Online Artifact* and was fiction guest editor for *Scissors and Spackle* in 2013 & 2014. Reese is currently Editor-in-Chief of the online magazine *MadHat Lit*, the quarterly online presence of MadHat Publishing. Reese won the first Patricia McFarland Memorial Prize for her flash fiction and The Graduate School Creative Writing Award from The University of Memphis for her poetry, where she earned her MFA. Reese won the 15th Glass Woman Prize in 2014 for her flash fiction and currently lives in Texas with six fine cats and three lovely men.